discovering. exploring. discovering. le...

discovering. exploring. discovering.

g. discovering.

learning. exploring. discovering. learning. exploring.

France

Children's travel activity and keepsake book

tinytourists
explore. discover. learn.

Bonjour !

Hello! My name's Topher*
and I love adventures!

I'll be keeping you company on your journey through
this book. Look out for me, I'll be popping
up every now and again.

Each time you see me, say
"bonjour" to say hello!

Count how many times
you can spot me...

*Topher is named after St. Chris**topher**, the patron saint for travellers who is famous for keeping all those who travel free from harm.

tinytourists is all about inspiring family travel and making the most of adventures; keeping travel meaningful and memorable, educational and fun. Visit us on Facebook to find out more and to join the tinytourists' community.

Written and Designed by Louise Amodio
Illustrated by Louise Amodio and Catherine Mantle
Cover Illustrations by Isabella (aged 4), Giacomo (8), Luca (6), George (8).

Published by Beans and Joy Publishing Ltd as a product from Tiny Tourists Ltd, Great Britain.
www.beansandjoy.com

ISBN: 978-0-9954949-1-6

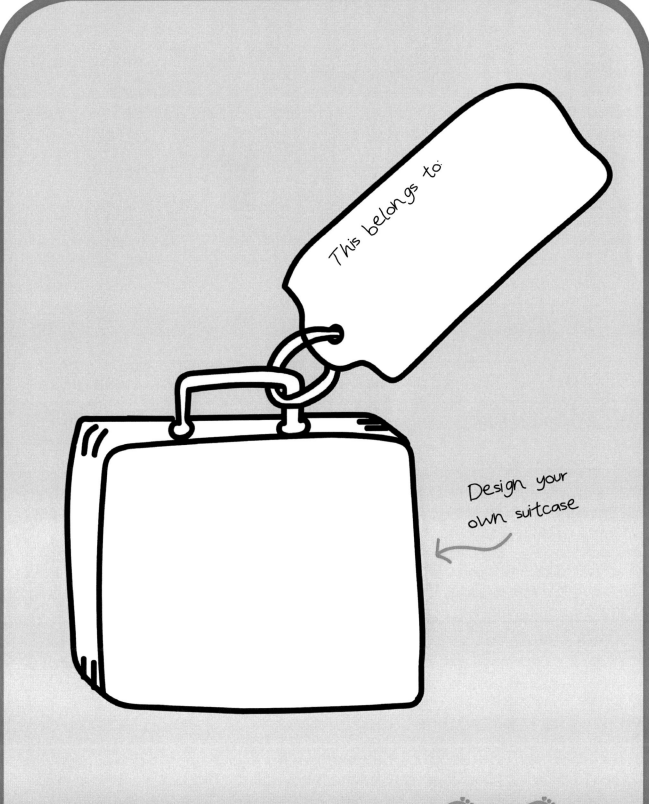

This belongs to:

Design your own suitcase

Your adventure starts here

How to use this book

Welcome to your fun-packed travel activity book!

Look out for these symbols to tell you what type of activity you'll be doing so you can start to work independently:

 for drawing, writing and mark-making

 for colouring

Time to get started!

For the grown-ups to read:

Section 1: My Travel Log

Use this section to start thinking about your trip to France; when you're going, where you're going, who you're going with, what the weather be like, and what you'll pack in your suitcase. This will help form part of a lovely keepsake as well as practice your planning and organisational skills!

Section 2: Explorer Skills

This section is full of games and activities for a bit of France-themed fun. All are designed to support the National Curriculum and grouped into **Maths (p12-25)**, **Literacy (p26-36), and The World Around Us (p37-42)** . See index for details.

Also included are some french words you might like to try out during your trip. We give you the true spelling, the phoentic spelling, and the english translation to make things straightforward.

phrase: bonjour
say: (bon joor)
meaning: hello

phrase: merci
say: (mur si)
meaning: thank you

phrase: s'il vous plait
say: (seel voo play)
meaning: please

Section 3: Memory Bank

This is where you can record all the memories from your trip. The perfect finishing touch to a lovely book of holiday memories; what you did, what you ate, what you saw, what you collected, and fun lists for recording the best bits and the worst bits.

Happy Travels!

My Travel Log

Me:

Stick or draw your picture here →

My Destination:

Arrival:

Date: _____

Passport Stamp:

Departure:

Date: _____

Where am I going?

This is a map of France. The capital city of France is Paris.
Find out where you are going on holiday, any journeys you may
be taking, and add them to the map:

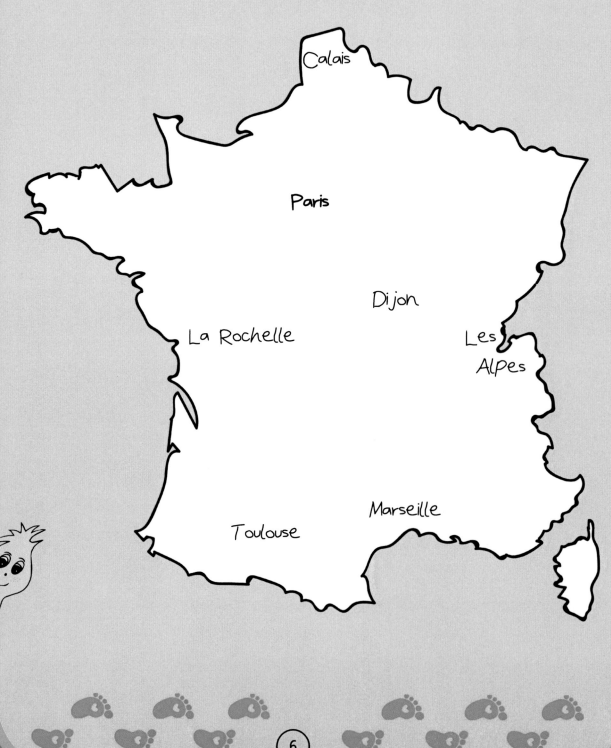

Calais

Paris

Dijon

La Rochelle

Les
Alpes

Marseille

Toulouse

How will I get there?

Find the transport you're using to get to France and colour them in:

What am I taking with me?

Draw the important things you've got packed in your suitcase:

Mon sac
(mon sack)
My bag

Who am I going with?

Draw a picture of who you're going on holiday with in the frame below:

Example

Holiday Portrait

Ma maman	Mon papa	Mon frere	Ma soeur	Mes grand-parents
(ma mamon)	(mon papa)	(mon frair)	(ma sur)	(mes grond-paronts)
My mummy	My daddy	My brother	My sister	My grandparents

What will the weather be like?

Draw a circle around the weather you think you'll have:

Il pleut
(eel pl)
It's raining

Il fait beau
(eel fay bow)
It's sunny

Il neige
(eel nej)
It's snowing

Explorer Skills

Maths

Literacy

The World
Around Us

Le Tricolore

Colour in the french flag below using blue and **red**:
How many flags can you spot on your travels?

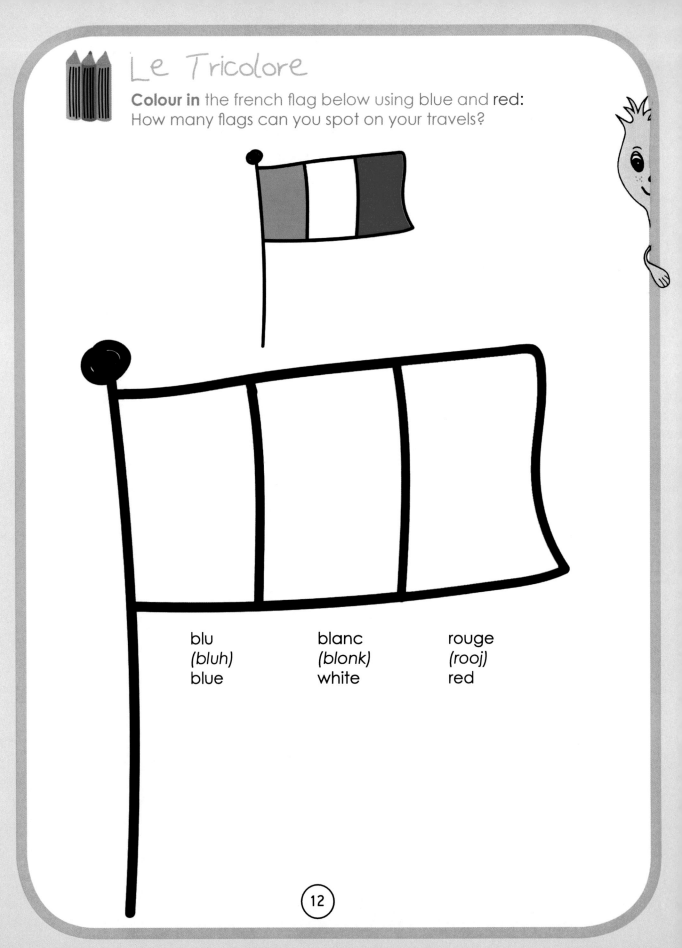

blu   blanc   rouge
(bluh)   *(blonk)*   *(rooj)*
blue   white   red

Paintbrushes

France is famous for its many artists. You can sometimes see them on the street painting people or objects. They might use charcoal, chalks or paint. Have you spotted any?

Can you **circle** all the **blue** paintbrushes below? How many are there?

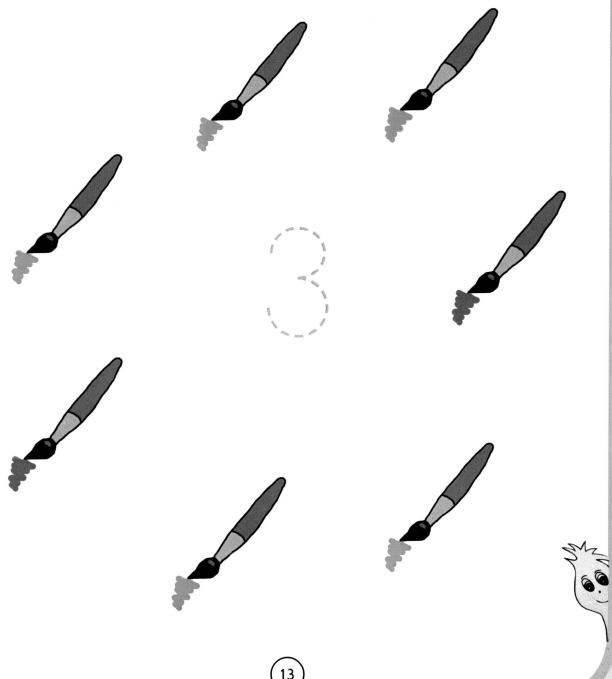

Paintbrushes

Circle all the **red** paintbrushes.
How many are there?

Waterlillies

One was of France's famous artists was called **Claude Monet** and one of his paintings was of a bridge and a pond full of waterlillies. It is worth millions of pounds!

Try to **colour in your own painting** of a bridge and some colourful waterlillies. You might like to add some water too.

Boulangerie 1-5

A french bakery is called a boulangerie (boo-lon-jeri). They sell all types of bread and pastries.

Count the items in this boulangerie and circle the right number:

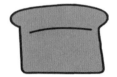

1 2 3 4 5

du pain
(du pan)
bread

1 2 3 4 5

un croissant
(un quasan)
a croissant

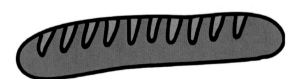

1 2 3 4 5

une baguette
(oon bagette)
a french stick

1 2 3 4 5

pain au raisin
(pan o raisan)
raisin pastry

Helping in the Boulangerie 1-10

Every morning fresh bread is baked in the boulangerie.

Help the owner of the boulangerie **count** how much bread he has made today:

   1 2 3 4 5 6 7 8 9 10

   1 2 3 4 5 6 7 8 9 10

   1 2 3 4 5 6 7 8 9 10

    1 2 3 4 5 6 7 8 9 10

un	deux	trois	quatre	cinq	six	sette	huit	neuf	dix
un	*der*	*twar*	*cat*	*sank*	*sees*	*set*	*wheat*	*nerf*	*deese*
1	2	3	4	5	6	7	8	9	10

Fromage 1-5

Cheese is another very popular food in France.
French people call it fromage and it is sold in a fromagerie.
Have you tried any?

Count the cheeses in this fromagerie and circle the right number:

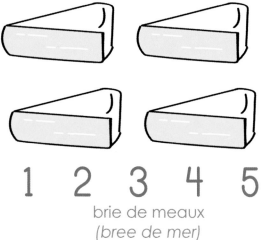

1 2 3 4 5

brie de meaux
(bree de mer)

1 2 3 4 5

roquefort
(rock-for)

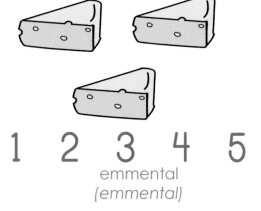

1 2 3 4 5

emmental
(emmental)

1 2 3 4 5

camembert
(camembear)

fromage
(fromaj)
cheese

fromagerie
(fromajeri)
cheese shop

Helping in the Fromagerie 1-10

Using your counting skills, help the owner of the fromagerie to **count** up her cheeses:

      1 2 3 4 5 6 7 8 9 10

1 2 3 4 5 6 7 8 9 10

1 2 3 4 5 6 7 8 9 10

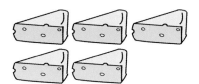

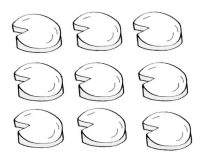   1 2 3 4 5 6 7 8 9 10

Snail Fun

In France, some people enjoy eating cooked snails! They are called Escargot *(escargo)* and are often cooked in butter and a herb called parsley. Do you think you would like to try one?

Colour in these snails with your favourite colours and patterns:

20

Picnic Matching Pairs

Help prepare a picnic for two people by matching all the pairs to make sure you have enough food.

Draw a line from one food to another food that is the same to match the pairs :

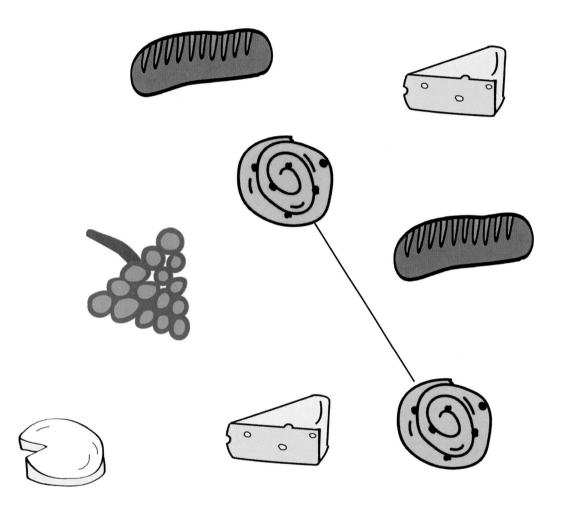

King of the Mountains!

Every July there is a big bike race through France called **Le Tour de France**. It takes 3 weeks from beginning to end and during the race the cyclists have to go up and down some mountains. The cyclist best at cycling through the mountain stages of the race wins the title "King of the Mountains".

Look carefully at this mountain.
Can find the **smallest** bike on the mountain?

bicyclette
(bichyclett)
bicycle

Petite!

Can you circle the **smallest** bicycle in each row:

petite
(peteet)
small

Skiing in France

France has many mountains which people love to ski down.

Look carefully at this mountain.

Can you find the **biggest** skier on this ski slope:

Grande!

Can you circle the **biggest** skier on each slope?

grande
(grond)
big

Arc de Triomphe

The Arc de Triomphe is a very important building in Paris - the capital city of France - that was built to remind people about the brave soldiers that fought in the wars to protect France. It is surrounded by a huge roundabout with lots of cars.

Use your colouring pencils to **add some colour** to this picture, and maybe add some cars:

Tour de Eiffel

The Eiffel Tower is France's most famous monument. It was built to celebrate the French Revolution. It has some pretty fountains in front of it, and a very long garden called Jardin de Tuileries.

Use your colouring pencils to **add some colour** to this picture and maybe add some ponds and fountains, grass and flowers:

FACT! **The Eiffel Tower has 1,700 steps up to the top (but there is also a lift)**

Le Louvre

In Paris, there is a famous art gallery called **Le Louvre**.
The entrance is a huge pyramid shape made of glass.

Can you **find your way** through this maze from the underground
train station (**Le Metro**) to the art gallery entrance:

The Mona Lisa

Inside Le Louvre art gallery are lots of famous paintings; of people, places and interesting things. One of the most famous paintings is of a lady called **Mona Lisa** who has a curious smile.
It is worth millions of pounds!

Colour in this outline of the Mona Lisa and then create your own smiley-faced masterpieces in the other frames:

Notre Dame Cathedral

In Paris, there is a famous cathedral, called **Notre Dame**. This is the setting for the famous story "The Hunchback of Notre Dame" in which a bell-ringer falls in love with a beautful dancer called Esmeralda.

Find your way through this maze from the underground train station (**Le Metro**) to the cathedral:

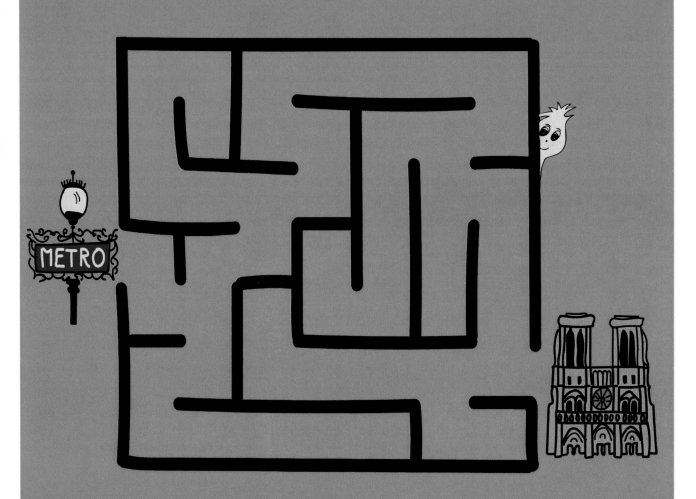

The Bells

The Hunchback of Notre Dame's job was to look after and ring the cathedral bells.

Trace around the outline of these bells and add some colours and patterns to make them look special:

Frere Jacques

Another story involving church bells is told in the nursery rhyme of Frere Jacques - a monk who is supposed to ring the church bells but has fallen asleep.

Guess what will happen when the bells start to ring?

Frere Jacques, Frere Jaques
Dormez-vous? Dormez-vous?
Sonnez les matines, sonnez les matines
Ding ding dong, ding ding dong

Frere Jacques colouring

Complete this picture of Frere Jacques using your own choice of colours:

 Are you sleeping, are you sleeping?
Brother John, Brother John?
Morning bells are ringing, morning bells are ringing
Ding ding dong, ding ding dong

Shape-search

Find the objects in this grid that look like circles and triangles. How many are there? Do you recognise any other shapes?

 _____  _____

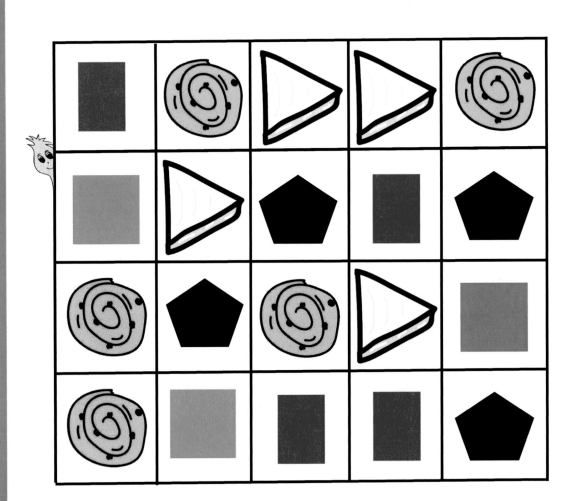

Letter search - France

Find as many of these 3 letters in the grid as you can:

f_ c _ a_

f	r	a	n	a
r	c	f	c	n
e	n	a	f	e
a	f	f	c	f

Write your name in the sand

France is surrounded by 2,000 miles of coastline along it's North, Atlantic and Mediterranean coasts, with sandy beaches, rocky beaches and cliffs and tiny coves.

Can you add some shells, sandcastles, and parasols to this beach, and **write your name** in the sand?

Ice-creams at the beach

Do you like ice-cream? In each row of ice-creams below try to spot the one that's different and draw a circle around it:

une glace
(oon glas)
an ice-cream

Chateaux spot the difference

In France, there are many beautiful palaces.
You may spot, or even visit one on your travels.

See if you can spot the **5 differences** between these two palaces:

un chateau
(un shattoe)
a palace

A Place to Stay

Where are you staying on your holiday in France? Is it a hotel?
A house? A tent? A boat? A chateau? Something else?

Can you draw a picture of it here?

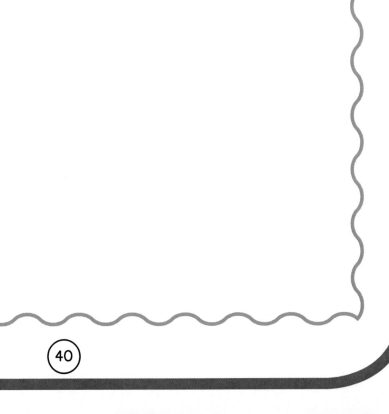

Home Sweet Home

Can you draw a picture of where you live back at home?

What is different about this and your holiday home?

What can you remember?

Can you circle some of the things you might see in France?
Which things do you think you might NOT see in France?

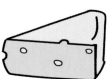
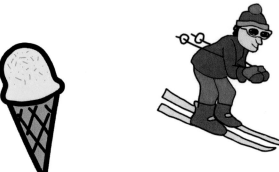

Memory Bank

Use this section to record and remember all the
things you've done, seen and tasted on your trip!
Draw, Write, Staple, Stick!

You may need a grown up to
help with some of the writing...

What have you eaten?

Draw some food you have eaten on holiday on the plate below. What was your favourite?

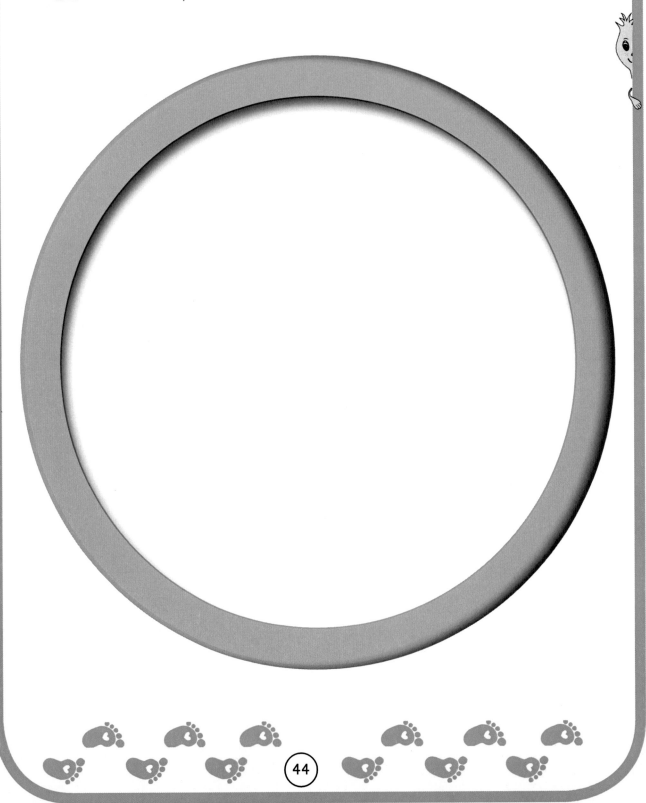

What adventures have you had?

Ask someone to help you write a postcard about your adventures, and design a nice stamp:

Carte Postale

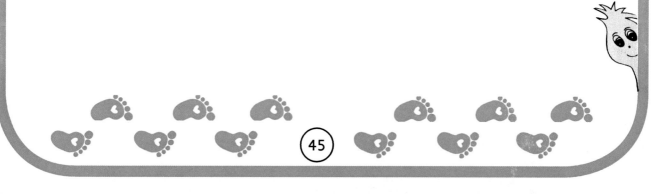

Momento Collage

Stick bits and pieces on these pages that you've collected during your trip; favourite tickets, receipts, leaflets, drawings, flowers...

Daily Diary

Note down some of the different things you have done each day:

Monday

Tuesday

Wednesday

Thursday

Friday

Saturday

Sunday

Memory Gallery

Draw pictures or doodles of any special memories:

Top 5

What have been the **best** five things about your trip?

_____

_____

_____

_____

_____

Worst 5

What have been the **worst** five things about your trip?

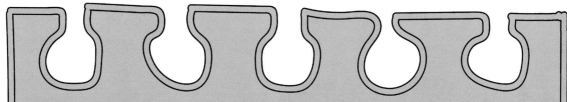

_____

_____

_____

_____

_____

Index

(what's in this book and where you can find it)

Au revoir !

(Good-bye, until next time)

I hope you enjoyed your adventure and completing this book along the way.

How many times did you spot me?

_____

Where would you like to go next?

Spain

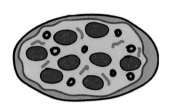

Italy

Greece

USA

Egypt

China

UK

Australia

Kenya

Thailand

Mexico

Finland

Made in the USA
Las Vegas, NV
08 May 2023

71751535R00033